Somebody Soup

Poems By
Abria M. Smith

Copyright © 2019 by Abria M Smith.

ISBN: Softcover 978-0-578-57350-2

All rights reserved. No part of this book may be reproduced or transmitted in any form or by any means, electronic or mechanical, including photocopying, recording, or by any information storage and retrieval system, except by a reviewer who may quote brief passages in a review to be printed in a magazine or by a newspaper, without permission in writing from the copyright owner.

Printed in the United States of America

Writhm
writhm.com
everythingwrithm@gmail.com

For every somebody who made me feel something.

Contents

1   Somebody Soup

Somebody Lost

5   Is There a Way?
6   Dead Inside
7   "Two Weeks"
8   BabyDaddy
10 Assimilation
11 Frigid Heart
12 Brother, Please

and Found

15 See Me
16 I Laugh
17 Granny
18 When My Baby Dances . . .
20 Lady Amaretto
21 So What, it's Mine
22 Try Again?
23 Can I Tell Him I Love Him?
24 I am Love
25 Dream Come True
26 I Tried to Write a Love Song
27 Pushed Back to Strength

Somebody Sensual

31 Something
32 Sweet Lovin'
33 Don't Wanna Love You
34 Riding
35 I Had a Dream
37 My Reality
38 Untitled
39 You Can't Quench This Thirst
40 Again Tonight
41 Last First Kiss
42 Both of You

and Proud

47 Queen
48 Black . . . What is That?
49 Sublime Rhyme

Somebody Faithful

53 What Mama Say
54 Given a Chance
55 Search
56 Angels
57 Mama's Love
58 Behind the Glass
59 Edea
60 Absalom
61 Your Glory

62 You, Brother
64 Guitar
65 Treasure
66 Hoping
67 Show Whatcha Got

Somebody Spoken

71 Deadlines
72 Voice
74 Saturday
75 Romie, No!
76 My Ideal Man
77 Heal
78 Can You?
80 Gettin' Paid
81 She Creates
82 To the Core
83 Heart and Mind
84 Amar's Dedication
85 Special
86 Happiness
87 Forever Yours
88 Did I . . .
89 Jazz History
91 Tasty
92 Service
94 Condensed Me

Somebody Else's Soup

Somebody Soup

Longing for something to nourish my soul.
Hungry for food that will make me feel whole.
Sick of the junk that just gets me by.
Somebody Soup is the new thing I'll try.
I tasted life and it did me no good.
Spent too much time feeling misunderstood,
Not understanding what held me back.
Somebody Soup was the thing that I lacked.
Wasting my days being stuck, feeling lonely.
Hurt and dismayed by the ones who disowned me.
Dreaming, not living, pasts worth reminiscing.
Somebody Soup was the thing I was missing.
So I took my tears and, with self-love, I mixed them.
Threw in some problems and strength to help fix them.
Created a dish that's bitter and hearty—
Somebody Soup, to make me somebody.

Somebody Lost

Is There a Way?

Is there a way to say and not say what you feel?
To fictionalize what's undoubtedly real?

Is there a way to be truthful and not be sincere?
To weep with elation and not shed a tear?

Is there a way to convey and not to impart?
To speak from ones soul and not from the heart?

Is there a way to strengthen and not to make stronger
To wish for forever and not ask for much longer?

Dead Inside

I've grown tired of playing this
tedious game.
Disguising my sorrow, concealing
my pain.
Shielding my soul with a
fallacious grin.
Attempting to disclaim this torment
I live in.
My heart wants to love, but my soul
fears rejection.
I'm caused to be callous by
lack of affection.
Dejected and drained from the tears
that I've cried,
Devoid of emotion,
I'm dead inside.

Two Weeks"

"Two weeks" was a joke
When I broke all my rules
And I soaked in my pools of fools' tears.
And for years,
Well-hidden grief reappeared.

"Two weeks" was a game
With the same pointless goal
And the pain would pierce holes in souls, deep.
I'd weep,
For I never sowed what I reaped.

Now, "Two weeks" is a chance
When I glance in his eyes
And I dance, high on sighs of sheer pleasure.
No measure
Is there for this newly found treasure.

"Two weeks" is a dream
One that just gleams so bright
And it just seems too right, I fight-scared
Unprepared
To end the two weeks that we've shared.

BabyDaddy

BabyDaddy.
He wears the title like a badge that
Proves his manhood.
Yeah, he played the game
And he ain't ashamed that he made
A child that don't know his name.

He don't have time to waste
On diapers, first teeth and doctor's visits.

He lets the mama do that.

BabyDaddy.
Brags to his boys about
The seeds he has planted.
But he made it clear
That he won't shed a tear if his seeds are aborted
And never make it here.

He don't have money to waste
On bottles, food or baby clothes.

He lets the state do that.

BabyDaddy.
He laughs as he swears that he won't
be tied down.

He keeps living lies
And runs as he tries not to see his own sadness
In his baby's eyes.

He don't have time to waste
on being a father to his child.

He lets a real man do that.

Assimilation

They rise from barren topsoil and concrete
In the midst of crime spattered tenements,
Where hope's faint cries are often muffled and muted
By the bellowing roars of ignorance.

Escape is a journey through unseen barriers.
Electric waves of light exposing new
Knowledge and levels of consciousness to the
"privileged" ones.
Those whose dark chocolate phonics can be
Gradually transformed to alpine white
Vernacular that others comprehend.

Frigid Heart

A frigid heart can find spring
Cascading into delicious pools,
Filling life with liquid joy
From beauty veneered vessel.

In trust's light blooms seeds
Once planted and forgotten amongst
The withered buds of hope from
Winters past.

It floats on warm waves
Into summer's intoxicating heat
Fueled by empty promises.
Promises that flutter like wings
On baby birds learning to fly,
Not anticipating the fall
Which inevitably cools
Into winter.

Brother Please

Brother please consider this,
While hearts you break and then dismiss.
Selfish games, for your gratification, you play.
A slave to your temptations.
To you, worth goes unrecognized
As you judge beauty with your eyes.
Emotions are life but, in your heart, dead
As you're lead by the will of an unconscious head.
You can't be whole when detached from your feelings,
Or until you are righteous in all of your dealings.
And learn to acknowledge the feelings of others,
Respecting your sisters as both wives and mothers

Brother please realize how special you are,
Though from home you've traveled far.
And the greater part of your ancestors' pride
Was lost with the truth that your captors still hide.
And yet, your seed holds so much power.
Strength from which most others cower.
But you would let them rule your earth,
Deserting your queens as they give birth.
And treating the worst, those who love you the best,
Failing repeatedly God's simple test.
You he has chosen-his soldier of beauty.
The truth is your light,
So make that your duty.

and
Found

See Me

See Me.
Eyes of Emerald
Soul of coal
Heart of granite, past untold.
Dreams of youth, mind of old
Don't ask what my future holds
Just see me.

I Laugh

I laugh, though my heart is filled with sorrow.
I dream, though my eyes see not tomorrow.
Above scorn, deceit and treachery
I soar on wings of lace.
No envy, greed or malice within.
No mask to shield my face.
Words, false witness they may bear,
But hearts, lies cannot tell.
For those who live within my heart
Are those who know me well.

Granny

Who has earned the name that power adorns?
With rose like beauty, occasional thorns.
Called upon by family, friends and those she met.
Studied her family, lest they forget
That no one can make it alone.
She sent what she could to care for family back home.
And with strength in her heart, offered love, tough as nails.
Through her stern, caring guidance it's her love that prevails.
Who's willing to sacrifice, give her last dime?
When beckoned, respond, and arrive just in time.
Who is most understanding, yet least understood?
Sometimes seen badly while intending good.
Loving and nurturing, though rough she can be.
She is the one known to loved ones as Granny.

When My Baby Dances..

I love to watch my baby dance,
His subtle strength and class.
He steps and my heart aches.
He turns and my soul shakes.
He leaps and, as his earth, I quake.

When my baby dances
His arms flow with the grace
Of wings on black butterflies.

His hands, opened wide, welcome me.

When my baby dances
He dances for freedom,
And his feet dance the march of
A million black soldiers.

I love to watch my baby dance,
His passionate expression.
He sways and I'm mesmerized.
He bends and I'm hypnotized.
He winds and tears fall from my eyes.

When my baby dances,
His eyes glow with the embers of
Radiant black love.

His succulent flesh beckons me.

When my baby dances,
He dances for life.
And he moves to the beat of
Eternity.

Lady Amaretto

Her style, her stride, so fine.
The way she talks, divine.
She's seen the faces, been to the places.
Lady Amaretto

Her skin as smooth as marble,
Her frame intense and narrow,
Her countenance is stolid
With eyes of wary sparrow.

She's the one you see at night,
The one who makes you wonder.
Will she dissemble innocence,
Conceal her plan for plunder?

She is the lady. She's earned her name,
Lady Amaretto.
She's learned to survive, how to stay alive
In the unforgiving ghetto.

So What, it's Mine

I don't buy the lye that tells me that my hair
should be straight.
I'm straight with my hair the way it is.

Black is not a fashion statement, some passing fad,
the latest trend.
I won't fry my hair to be someone else
Until it's ok to be black again.

I wanna wash and go, twist my locks, let them flow.
Happy, nappy and proud.
Some may not like it
But so what, it's mine.

Try Again?

I must admit I'd like to try
To solve the mystery of those eyes
That seem to see right through the outer me.
While exposed, I'm transposed
To keys I never though I'd know.
I sing of giving love reluctantly.
Can I trust again while I lust again?
Should I feel again while you reel me in?
Is your game the same? Will I feel the shame?
Is this the same thing from our past renamed?
Not wanting to love but my heart knows no better.
Drowning in feelings, I hide behind letters.
Writing out words when I tried
To pour out my heart when my mind was tongue-tied.
So eager to care, but reluctant to fall.
Scared to give in while I'm giving my all.
Admitting my love but denying that I'm in it.
Running this race but unsure if I'll win it.

I don't wanna be a fool. But these feelings.
I don't wanna play the games. But it seems right.
I won't make the same mistakes. But I think I'm falling in . . .

You mess up this time and that's it.

Can I Tell him I Love Him?

Can I tell him I love him
And be sure that he knows
That this love that I feel is unique
That never before have I felt what I feel
Nor uttered the words that I speak

Can I tell him I love him
from my soul to his
And make sure that he understands
A love of this nature can only exist
As something the universe plans

Can I tell him I love him
without expectation
Or need for reciprocal shows
Of this infinite love that envelops my soul
Can I tell him

He already knows

I am Love

I need love
I breathe love
I give love
I live love
I take love
I make love
I can love
I AM love

Dream Come True

I struggle in vain to catch my breath, tired.
You have me winded, yet I'm inspired
By you, whom I've chased through the fields of my dreams,
Where innocence blushes in cool, joy-filled streams.
I'd imagine how your soul would feel to me
If one day it somehow became real to me.
These visions I've had, these thoughts, bittersweet
Since I've doubted the chances that we'd ever meet.
Now finally I've reached my fantasy's end.
No longer a dream, but a possible friend.

I Tried to Write a Love Song

I tried to write a love song
To say what's in my heart,
How everything I've ever known
means less when we're apart.

I tried to hum a melody,
A theme for our romance,
From our first chance encounter
To this blessed circumstance.

I tried to find the perfect chords
Composed in perfect time,
To show how wonderful it feels
When your hand rests in mine.

I tried to keep the loving tones
Contained within the staff,
To imitate the lovely tones
Contained within your laugh.

I tried and failed to write
What only hearts can comprehend.
Unlike our love, words are defined
And every song must end.

Pushed Back to Strength

You've disparaged me with words, yet I thrive.
You've tried to break my spirit, but I'm still alive.
You drain me of emotion, yet I give.
You burn my soul in your personal hell,
but miraculously, it lives
And forgives.

Asserted that you could control me, but could you?
Said you'd always devise some way to hold me,
but would you?
You've forced me and pushed me
Days endless in length,
But through torment and anguish I'm pushed
Back to strength.

Somebody Sensual

Something

I don't know what it is, but there's something
That makes few words say so much
And adds heat to an innocent touch.
I know that there is something.

Not quite sure about it, but there's something
That makes goodbye a tragic song
And makes the time away seem long.
I'm sure of the fact that there's something.

I've tried to ignore it, but there's something
That countless poems and songs inspires
And fuels imagination's fires
I cannot ignore that there's something

Sweet Lovin'

Sweet lovin',
Never had it so good.
Don't even think I ever dreamed
That I could.

It smells just like summer,
The flowers in June.
Like a fresh flowin' river on a
Hot afternoon.

It feels like the autumn,
A soft blowin' breeze,
Like the gentle caress of the sun
On the trees.

It tastes like the winter,
A snowflake in flight,
And flickering fire on a cold
Silent night.

But it looks like the birth,
Which takes place in the spring.
Sweet love.
Love so sweet,
It could be anything.

Don't Wanna Love You

Wanna ride the soft waves of laughter in your smile,
Bathe in the cream of your sultry voice,
Touch your soul, which brings me hope
But I don't wanna love you.

Wanna know those eyes that see right through me,
Kiss those lips that constantly tempt me,
Taste the flesh that holds sweet pleasures
But I don't wanna love you.

Wanna be held captive in those strong, yet gentle arms,
Be enveloped by the heat of your touch,
Lose myself in the flames you ignite
Still, I don't wanna love you.

Yet, I do.

Riding

I remember so clearly, riding,
Barely able to breathe.
Holding you.
Squeezing your hips between my thighs.
Safe.
For you only move as quickly as I desire.
And my pulse quickens
As I experience the pleasure
Of riding for the first time
With you.

I Had a Dream

I had a dream last night that felt so alive
I asked the question, "How real is reality?"
I dreamed a dream so vivid with colors cascading,
Bathing my words in sensuality
As they flowed from my mouth in your direction.
An arrow to a bull's eye as to you my affection.
And you looked at me and smiled
As the brilliance of passion in your eyes ran wild.
I became your song,
And as I flowed from your lips,
The taste of the melody burned in my hips.
And I drifted
Engulfed in the rapture of your touch.
I was dreaming,
But nothing had ever thrilled me so much
As this fantasy, into which you came.
I invited your touch as you sang me.
I lost my breath as I gave in and shared my soul,
Finding love in a fantasy.

I had a dream last night and I swore it was real
Because consciousness lingered so near.
Tangled in emotions I felt from within,
But the farthest away was fear.
Like lava that flows boils cool water,
So burned my love, only hotter.

In the heat of my passion, I died in your lap,
A death I would relish again.
To die in a dream with you by my side
Is such an enticing end.
It's too sweet to be fiction, yet perfect—unreal.
Words can't describe what it is that I feel.
I'd name this feeling, but what's in a name?
Would desire renamed still cut so deep?
Would I still toss and sigh and shiver
Having visions of you in my sleep?

My Reality

It was merely déjà vu, the day that I met you
For the beauty I know now, I already knew.
You've appeared times before
in the dark palace of my dreams,
Leaving my mind open to imaginative schemes
Of feeding you fruits as exotic as my passion,
And adorning your body in eccentric fashions.
And I'd give you my cup filled with nectars of pleasure,
And sing you my heart's songs that tell of the treasures
I've found in you, the mate to my soul,
Which long ago was half but finally made whole,
By you who have been, in my dreams, my ideal.
A vessel to hold the emotions I feel.
So I pour into you all the love that is in me.
My night and my day, you end and begin me.
I submit to you wholly in the dark of my dreams
And shiver just thinking how real you have seemed.
This image of love, I once could not fathom.
Mine in my dreams. While awake, I couldn't have him.
But confusion now threatens to shake my mentality
For the man of my dreams now invades my reality.

Untitled

Oh, I'd like to linger on your lips,
And as you spread me with your middle finger,
I'll restore the shiny satin that calls,
Yearning to be touched.

To caress your face gently is the dream of a lifetime.
Your hands knead me into the recesses
Of your beauty's center.
I shield you from the harshness around you.

Your knees and elbows invite me
To play deep within them
As I soften the arch of their journey.

I even love your hair.
Its tight kink coils around me,
But still, I groom and quench it.

Your body knows no discomfort,
For I sooth all love's frictions
And convert them into delight.

I am here when needed.
Always longing to be a part of you,
To cling to you.
Smoothing all that is rough . . .

I am Vaseline.

You Can't Quench This Thirst

See, I've tasted summer
And damn, it gets hot.
Folks sip on red Kool-aid trying to
Hit that spot.
But this summer I'm feelin'-
A season, it's not.
And juice can't quench this thirst I got.

This burn in me is like hell in July,
Tail of a comet, some nap straightenin' lye.
Got heat like hot grits
Spilled on cold feet.
Steam like that from hot yams
That got to cool before we eat.
Heat I feel can reveal all you think you are
But are not.
'Cause you can't quench this thirst I got.

Don't want no cool drink to make my heat fizzle.
Ice is nice—water's hotter.
Oil tends to sizzle.
Now if you look while mama cooks
And ain't got the nerve to put your hand in the pot,
Then you sure can't quench
This thirst I got.

Again Tonight

Again tonight we'll dance our last goodbye

As candles cast their glow, exposing wounds

From scrapes with déjà vu's cyclonic eye,

That tells a tale of soft caresses bruised.

Again tonight we'll sing our final cry.

The song repeats-our lives within the staff.

Where words' true meanings go unrecognized,

And once again we drink our final laugh.

Last First Kiss

Last first kiss
Vast, pursed bliss

Lips grasp, well met
Eclipsed, past regret

Pure, true, tender
Sure to remember

The last first kiss

Both of You

Heat intense, passion true.
One is enough, but there are two.
The first, through darkness shines.
Burning passion, undisguised.
I feel him. He feels me.
What I feel now is sweet ecstasy.
Filled to the top, yet longing for more.
So much to explore.
He kisses my lips and tastes my soul.
What once was half, with him, is whole.
He holds me close. Our minds are one.
Eternity has just begun.
I want to drown in desire.
Maybe that would quench this fire.

The other one,
Simply sweet.
The one that makes the love complete
If dreams don't lie, could this be real?
If love should hurt, is this pain I feel?
Finding heaven in his arms,
Lost in love that's in his eyes.
Intoxicating - that's his charm.
His love is real, wearing no disguise.

Two loves.
Not the same,
But still called by one name.
One fulfilling a physical need.
The other, providing mentally.
I am faithful in love.
Yet, still, I love two.
Never deceiving,
Both loves are you.

and

Proud

Queen

I am Queen.
From my womb emerged a race
With hair like wool upon each head,
Colorful satin on every face.
My eyes hold greatness,
My soul within.
Ears hear resounding glory.
Upsetting the course of history,
For truth is in
Her story.

Black .... What is That?

Black. What is that?
Is it the soot on papa's shirt?
Or is it the dirt in his fingernails?
Could it be the deep, dark tone of mama's voice?
Or is it her solemn eyes?
Maybe black is something else.
Sister says that black cats are bad luck.
So does that mean that black is evil,
That black belongs to the devil?
Is it that sinister shadow lurking in my closet,
Or is it the nothingness that swallows me when
I close my eyes?
Could it be the gloomy night?
Or perhaps a storm,
Or ashes?

No, none of that is black.
I know what black really is.
Black is me.
My soul is an eternal black,
but that's not bad.
Black is proud and strong.
Black is sweet meditation.
Black is calm.
Mama said that black is the color that
Nana saw when God carried
Her to heaven.
Black is all these things.
But most of all, black is good.
And Lord, I'm proud to be black.

Sublime Rhyme

Sublime rhyme, spoken word in time.
Ebonics—Chocolate phonics to melodic lines.
Digging deep to touch roots where rhythm was grounded,
Rounded.
An oblate spheroid.
Hippin' and hoppin' and fillin' a void
In a galaxy that still attempts to deny that our complex rhythms that once rang on high still remain.
From beating our soul's drums we shall not refrain.
Our hearts beat in time. Those who rhyme are our Griots.
Oral historians ensuring that we know
from whence we came.
What's in a name?
Would a poet, renamed, still flow as sweetly?
And man, with homeland snatched from under his feet, be
Any less proud than if addressed by the name of his own kin?
For it is thought, not Geography, that determines
what state he's in.
State of mind made sublime by rhyme,
which transcends space and time.
Seek, and you will find some still trying.
Denying this rhyme sublime is yours and mine.
But their crimes we shall unwind as they rewind and rewind and rewind the rhyme
Trying to find in their minds
what the rhyme sublime is implying.
To them, "Rhymes just rhyme".
For them, that's fine.
But rhyme is not mine if it isn't sublime.
Sublime Rhyme.

Somebody Faithful

What Mama Say

Mama say rain gonna come.
Come down, come down rain.
Come and wash away my fear.
Take away my pain.

Mama say the sun the sun gonna shine.
Shine sun. Shine down on me
Bright and fine.
Warm my heart and soothe my mind.

Mama say the moon gonna glow.
Glow moon. Glow bright.
When I see your soft, pretty face
I know everything gonna be alright.

Mama say the wind gonna fly.
Fly wind, fly.
Blow away my tears on them lonely nights
When I cry.

Mama say the stars gonna twinkle.
Twinkle stars, like glass
When I see you shining there
I know the storm has passed.

Mama say the world gonna turn.
Turn world, and as you turn
The older I'll get, and the more I'll learn
That's what mama say.

Given a Chance

Given a chance, a bud of hope will bloom,
As do all living things when given room.

Given a chance, a friendship can grow
When you open your heart to someone you don't know.

Given a chance, inner beauty shines through
Those you once thought were so unlike you.

And given a chance, we can all be whole
If we judge with our minds less
And more with our souls.

Search

Is it wrong that I long for spiritual nourishment?
With no soul I'm not whole, but in need of encouragement.
Learning values from those who are so quick to judge.
They'd rather bruise than to lose,
Set in ways that won't budge.

Should I mimic the praises of "Church goin' black folk"?
And be led on a path by "Don't know what they lack" folk?
Or question the answers I'm led to believe,
And add truth I've sought to the knowledge received.

See, I'm on a quest.
At the end, what I shall find
Are solutions to problems that once plagued my mind.
I need a place where I feel it's alright to be me,
So I search in my home before God on my knees.

Angels

Since I was a lil' girl,
Angels been watching over me.

Long time ago when Pap Pap's fishin' boat
crashed on them rocks
And the dark water wrapped up 'round him like a blanket
That couldn't nobody find him in,
I asked them angels to save my Pap.
And they picked him up
and untangled him outta all that mess.
But don't nobody believe it was the angels.
They say Tommy Blue pulled ol' Pap out the water.

But I know it was the angels that done it
'Cause they tell me in my bed at night.
I know they gon' be here for me when I die
'Cause they promised to take me with them.

And now that I'm old, it feels good to know
Them angels been watching over me.

Mama's Love

I called out for mama, but she wasn't there,
And yet, I could still feel her presence.
It always felt like mama was there,
Even when she wasn't.
When I was lonely, I could close my eyes
And see mama's twinkling eyes.
Mama had the prettiest eyes,
The deepest green I've ever seen,
Like a calm sea.
In those gentle eyes, mama hid the secrets of her existence.
There was so much that yearned to know
About mama, but those same eyes that I took refuge in,
concealed what was inside mama.
What was mama feeling? I could never tell.
But I did know that mama loved me.
She didn't even have to say it.
Mama's love spoke for itself.
It was in her hands when she held me.
It was in her voice when she called my name.
And when mama would leave, it would stay with me.
I guess that's why when mama left,
I was never alone.

Behind the Glass

The NICU always seemed inviting when
I'd see my tiny child behind the glass,
In the glow of bilirubin light,
Amidst a vast entanglement of tubes
That breathed artificial life into my hopes.

This life that started on its course to soon
And slow blossomed from a fate unclear,
Does not remember those cribs with bars of steel.
Nor the sting of intravenous meds
Given to a child too weak to breathe.

I'd feed her through a nasogastric tube.
My breast milk, pumped for her, was liquid strength.
I watched her sleep, so hopeful she'd grow stronger.
Knowing not if I would have it in me
To help her grow and someday let her go.

Now once again I watch her through the glass
With ponytails and tales of what she'll learn.
Reluctantly, I leave the toddler class, knowing…
From here she'll grow, explore the world,
leave home and merely be
Behind the glass, a picture framed for me.

NICU – neonatal intensive care unit

Edea

Even though I've done this before
    Don't think that, at this parenting thing, I'm a pro
        Eventually I'll get it right with
            Another little girl to help me grow.

Absalom

Absolutely beautiful,
  Brother's baby boy.
    Surely you're a blessing,
      Always bringing joy.
        Love for you, we all possess.
          One sweet wish - you'll live no less than
            Many years of happiness.

Your Glory

Eyes that beam with strength of onyx,
Whose black intensity pierces the soul.

Lips, whose touch of satin shines
With honey coated splendor.

Valliant - you melt away the callous layers
Of a dormant heart
With disarming charm and healing embrace.

Bathe me in your summer
And I will fall as gently and swiftly
As an autumn leaf
Bowing down in the presence
Of your glory.

You, Brother

You, Brother.
You who have been stripped
Of all authority.
Replaced by monthly handouts in
Decapitated households.
Disrespected by your sisters
Who have been conditioned to be all else but
Submissive to your will.

You, Brother
You who have been cast out of a society
That refuses to teach the
True story of your worth.
Belittled for creating from a foreign civilization
A language and culture as colorful and unique as those
Which were stolen from you.
Ridiculed for adorning yourself in garments that express
Who you are, yet still creating culture that others wish to
emulate.

You, Brother
You who are sought after by
Women of all races,
Envied for the power that lies
In your hands-
Hands that not only defend with fists of might,

But also caress with palms of security.
Feared for the power contained by your seed
That grows and blooms
Deep in the wombs of your queens.

You, Brother.
You who are beautiful in mind, body and spirit.
Strong, sensitive, sensual.

You, Brother.
You who are cherished.

Guitar

He held the guitar close.

Back arched, fingers curled, he coaxed

A song from its strings;

A song that danced through the air like feathers

On the wind.

And the guitar sang sweetly of love

For the one whose hands gently caressed it.

I closed my eyes,

Attempting to claim the melody,

And imagined that I was this instrument,

Worthy of his caress

Treasure

If I needed one word to describe you,
Finding it would be a difficult task.
It's hard to describe such a beautiful heart
That gives freely without being asked.
For a spirit so caring and pure,
It's hard to choose only one word.
Or for a mind overflowing with wisdom
That can answer those questions unheard.
I'd search in vain, for mere words cannot measure
My beautiful friend - a valuable treasure.

Hoping

I see you
Even when I close my eyes.
Since we met
I've smiled at the thought of you.

It would be a lie if I tried to deny
That I fantasize.
'Cause the sound of your voice gives me butterflies.
But I'm taking my time
To read your soul, feel your mind.
To verify
That your shell has a core that can satisfy
The need in me
For warmth, wit and strong sensitivity
To coax me through storms when it rains.
And deep thoughts must run through your brain.
But I refrain from speaking
For seeking I am
Knowing not what I'll learn
Still I'm hoping, with time, that your friendship
I'll earn.

Show Whatcha Got

Mama, I wanna shine, but where do I start?
Got a dream in my mind
And a song in my heart.
If someone will listen, I'm willing to try
To capture a soul
Bring a tear to an eye.
If I were a diva, I'd offer a song.
But I can't hear the music.
My timing's all wrong.
And if I were an artist, I'd show off my style.
But I can't paint a picture
Of something worthwhile.
Not a gift do I have that will lead me to glory,
And nothing to tell
But a meaningless story.
But I can't stop striving. I'll struggle instead.
For in my heart, still
Are these words that you said:
"Even if you have nothing but a story to tell,
If you take the time to tell it,
Your time is spent well.
I love who you are.
You can't be who you're not.
What you don't have means nothing
Just
Show whatcha got"

Somebody Spoken

Deadlines

Deadlines.
    Looming above,
        Dangling from hair-like
    Strands of time.
Tickling the mind.
    Talking to the soul.
        Bringing to light
            What should have been done
            Before dark.

Voice

It rises from the depths of your innermost core
From places you've known, but not seen.
You've felt it, you've heard it, you've used it before
To converse and explain what you mean.

Defined as expressed opinion or choice,
Or sounds from the mouths of those living.
This beautiful gift I describe is your voice,
Both easy to share and worth giving.

How should it be used and what is the cost
For not realizing its might?
If it is abused, could it be lost?
And what can it do when used right?

Lifting a voice to rejoice and give praise
Should not be considered absurd.
Raising a voice when it needs to be raised
Can sometimes help one to be heard.

When used in song, it can be hypnotizing
Or healing with soothing words spoken.
It can pacify when violence is rising
Or repair a heart that's been broken.

When cleverly crafted, voiced words educate
And give the unseen shape and form.
When used to uplift, voice elevates
The victims of life's harshest storms.

To comfort a child, voice is the key.
A sweet lullaby it creates.
The use of ones voice should be planned carefully
As we live with the choices we make.

So, remember your strength. Learn to value your voice.
Forget not the day, nor the hour
When you first learned to use it. Be sure to rejoice
And know that, in voice, there is power!

Saturday

We danced.
Flesh upon flesh,
Our arms and legs followed
The paths of lover's limbs
In a pretentious waltz
Of eternity.

We embraced.
Hearts beating simultaneous measures.
Minds unaware of our detachment
From reality.

We kissed.
Our eyes, beneath closed lids,
Telling tales of splendor
Of which our souls were not convinced.

We woke.
Minds recovering
From lust's intoxication.
The faint dew of honey coated kisses
Still on our lips.

We parted,
Caressing with words laced with insincerity.
"Thank you. See you Saturday."

Romie, No!

Romeo, oh Romeo. Where the hell art thou, Romeo?
Where is my Romeo?
My sweet prince of the Ghetto?
You know, the one with the kisses tastin' like Amaretto.

Well, he ain't home.
I got a cheap imitation. His name is Jerome.
He lives on the corner of Copeland and 5th
And stays out all night with the boys talking shit.
Ain't got a job, says he's self employed.
When the cops come around he gets all paranoid.
The boy ain't got a pinch of romance.
Got two left feet and swear he can dance.
He don't take me out, likes to stay in for sex.
Damn five-minute brother keeps me askin', "What's next?"
Ain't got no car-always borrowin' mine.
When I need my ride I can't find his behind.
Done hollered at most of my girlfriends and cousins,
Then tries to lie saying, "Baby I wasn't."
My mama says he's trifling. My daddy just hates him.
I can't figure out why I started to date him.
Ain't seen him in days 'cause that fool owes me money.
The boy's like a joke that I don't think is funny.
So, next time I see him, I'll tell him where he can go.
To someone like him you best say, "Romie, No!"

My Ideal Man

My ideal man wants to get to know me.
He not only cares, but is willing to show me.
He isn't insensitive, callous nor cold.
He won't say he cares just to keep me on hold.
He cares what I think and he cares what I feel.
There's never a time when he wont "Keep it real".
He calls and explains when he can't be around
And realizes that, in me, treasure he's found.

My ideal man responds when I text him
And won't make me feel as if I've somehow vexed him.
He says what he feels and means each word that's said
Instead of placing false hopes in my head.
He cares for me, though all my faults he may see.
Around him I feel that it's safe to be me.
He doesn't mind that there are things that I lack.
And, best of all, my ideal man
Loves me back.

Heal

Let's heal together
Be real together
And maybe relearn
How to feel together

Can You?

I have yet to find a brother who can.
Can you?

I've heard a lot about how black folks
Just love themselves some chicken.
But when brothers see my chicken legs, it seems they be forgettin'
'Bout their craving for the poultry
So I'm saving my poetry for a brother who can.
Can you?

Can you love me before I get the Dr. Scholl's corn remover?
And with my unshaven bird legs, allow me to move ya?
Can you love me without any makeup?
Looking just as I do when I wake up?
See, I'm not like the girls in the videos
And may not have much as far pretty goes.
But can you?

Can you love me despite my not so tight belly?
I've been aiming for steel but my abs feel like jelly.
Can you look really deep and seek my inner beauty
And, instead of one ghetto, love my suburban booty?

'Cause I'm kinda different, share the mold of no other
But might not be picked first as wife or a lover.

Still, can you?
As I hide, in jest, my insecurities
Try to find more to explore in me?
Can you?

I have yet to find a brother who can.

Gettin' Paid

Gettin' Paid Gettin' paid Gettin' Paid,
I got it made in the shade cause I'm gettin' paid.

All the hottest clothes, I'm sportin'—gettin' paid
Folks trippin' off the shit they be snortin'—gettin' paid

Cruisin' in my expensive ride—gettin' paid
Obituary sayin' how another junkie died—gettin' paid

Buyin' all the top brand sound equipment—gettin' paid
The MAN denies all knowledge of the shipment—gettin' paid

Satin sheets on the bed where I'm lyin'—gettin' paid
Low birth weight crack babies are dyin'—gettin' paid

Providin' for self, fuck my brother—gettin' paid
Strung out, he robs his own mother—gettin' paid

Gettin' paid gettin' paid gettin' paid
I got it made in the shade cause I'm gettin' paid.

But damn, what a mess I made gettin' paid.

She Creates

Piercing her heart,
She bleeds on the page,
Crimson notes comprised
Of passion and rage.
Drained by her art,
And, yet, she persists.
If she ceased to create
Then she'd cease to exist.

To the Core

Don't love with the eye
for beauty soon fades

Don't love for the passionate
rush of love made

Don't love for possessions
you'll soon be without

Love to the core
from the inside out

Heart and Mind

I've got a glass half full heart
And a glass half empty mind.
The struggle is real
But worth it, most times.

Amar's Dedication

Slowly realizing what it means to be
Without the thing I'm longing for.
But I will long for more
Until I find that which fills my cup, and fill it up.

My anticipation boils and overflows
And grows as it shows me
It is a many splendored thing.
My mind's bells ring.
And swift melodic thoughts
Make my heart sing.

Quickly analyzing all the paths to take to get
To what I'm longing for,
So that I long no more.
When I find that missing part, my counterpart.

My imagination rises and shines
And winds as it reminds me
What I once knew so well
My mind can't tell.
For love, like sweet ambrosia,
Has cast its spell.

Special

You think that I'm special?
I am, so you should.
But my bad is as bad
As my good is good.

Happiness

If I've ever cared for you
Then I want you to be happy
Whether it's with or without me.
It isn't my job to make you feel happy
It's something you must choose to be.
I hope that you wish me happiness too
And that you won't think me unkind
For severing ties when I realize that
Yours comes at the expense of mine.

Forever Yours

Forever yours, for as long as I live,
I'll give to you all of the love I can give.
Forever yours, until the end of time,
No love for you will ever be greater than mine.
Forever yours, until death do us part,
There will always be a place for you in my heart.
Forever yours, these words I've inscribed
Were written to make you realize
I am forever yours.

Forever yours, my love for you
Will be everlasting and also true.
Forever yours, as the seasons change,
My love for you will always remain.
Forever yours, as day becomes night,
Loving you will be my heart's delight.
Forever yours, this loving refrain
Was written to help me to explain
I am forever yours.

Did I . . .

Did I wait?
Did I wonder?
Did I worry?
Did I suspect?
Did I impatiently watch the time?
Did I pretend to sleep as you crept in and showered?
Did I feel you slide into bed next to me?
Did I then sleep?

Did I wake?
Did I lie still?
Did I fear?
Did I ache?
Did I silently prepare your breakfast?
Did I see you off to work?
Did I do your laundry?
Did I smell a fragrance that I don't wear?
Did I then know?

Did I cry?
Did I scream?
Did I curse?
Did I ponder?
Did I solemnly make a decision?
Did I write the letter?
Did I make the telephone call?
Did I pack all of my belongings?
Did I leave you?
Did I.

Jazz History

On the history of jazz, class is now in session.
Gotta pay attention so you'll catch the lesson.
Don't be distracted while the lesson commences 'cause
Jazz is like a trip engaging all your senses.
Well, our first stop is Africa where complex rhythms
Were central to the lives of all of those who lived them.
Here, jazz's first heartbeat started with a drumbeat
That influenced the cultures it would meet.
These African rhythms traveled with African people, see.
The world of music changed dramatically.
In the West Indies, influenced by French and the Spanish,
The polyrhythmic beats were much too strong to vanish.
They mixed with the flavor of other cultures around
And soon began to form a jazzy sound that came from
Ragtime, Brass band music and Blues,
Spirituals, Minstrel and work songs too.

African rhythm survived American Slave trade
And out of it some new song forms were made,
Like field hollers and work songs to pass the time.
They became the Blues and then the rhythm went Ragtime.
In New Orleans it picked up Creole flavor,
Sophisticated brass bands for your ears to savor.
Mixed with the freestyle of freed slaves
Who, by ear, from their heads played songs
Marched in bands for those who passed on - no sad songs.

Then it moved to Chicago where improvisation grew
From being used as embellishment
into something brand new.
Then, in New York, the rhythms played quite symphonic,
Opening up the world of jazz harmonics.
Through much transformation was born what we know as
This cultural marriage called jazz.
Swing, Bebop, cool jazz, a wide array
Fusion, neoclassical—they're here to stay.

Tasty

If I licked the inside of your mind with the tip of my soul,
Would your insecurities slide out your left ear and leave a slippery trail across your shoulder?

Can I taste you in all those places that reject light,
Then shine into your darkness until I blind your senses?

When I suck your emotions and reach your core, what flavor will it be?

I know . . .

I'll call it tasty.

Service

If I were to serve you,
What would I do?
Would I welcome you warmly
And ask, "May I help you?"

Or would I salute,
Off to fight for the nation
And lay down my life
Without hesitation?

I could serve up a meal
As quickly as I'm able,
Then bid you adieu
Before I clear the table.

Or would I wear a badge,
Sworn to protect and serve?
Keeping the peace
While keeping my nerve.

There are so many visions
To mind service brings.
But maybe to serve
Is a whole different thing.

Do I not serve
When I help you to dream?
And help you see things
Aren't as tough as they seem.

And does it not serve you
When we work as one
To solve both our problems
And get our jobs done?

And is it not service
When, to you, I listen
And find out the best way
To fulfill our mission?

Condensed Me

I'm hungry for life and the feeling of wholeness.
Tired of feeling empty.
I need to fill myself with nourishing thoughts that soothe my soul.

Don't feed me lines to take my mind off what I really need.
I want to feel complete, from the inside out.
I want that "stick to your ribs" type of sustenance that can't be bought in stores.

I want to be filled to the point where I feel I need no more,
And then some.
Wanna be alone without feeling lonely
And learn to be my own best friend.

But first I have to purge myself of all the junk
The world has fed me.
I don't need it anymore.
I can strip myself of all that isn't me.

I'm gonna simmer myself over the seething heat of
Trials and tribulation, collect the
Vapors of my soul and drink a bowl of
Condensed me.

Somebody Else's Soup

Delphinic Dimensions

By John H. Redd III

In the brightest corner of my mind
There's a place that I know well.
It's a place of warmth and tenderness
a place reserved for Del.

It's a place of pure enchantment
Where other eyes can't see.
And no one walks along its roads
Except for Del and me.

The paths are strewn with roses
With butterfly and bee
And there our names appear within,
A heart on every tree.

A note to other lovers
Who've tried at love and fell,
Cultivate your land of dreams
And love as I love Del.

Shining Star

By Joseph Smith

Shining star, shining so bright
It looks like you have given birth to the night.
It flitters and flashes to the earth.
It is so beautiful. How much is it worth?

There is so much beauty you couldn't pay the price.
But it is nice
And made for me and you to enjoy
And give to our girls and our boys
Not to destroy but also enjoy.

Shining star, shining so glorious
I know that you were meant for all of us.
You shine and glow in the summer and in the winter snow.
Such beauty, I am glad it can't be sold
And that we can only behold.

So shine on and light the night.
Your beauty is always right.
It blends and brings a lovely night.

I am, Yet I am Not

By Sheiry Smith

I am big, yet I am small.
I am smart, yet I am dumb.

I am soft, yet I am callous.
I am happy, yet I am sad.

I live in one world, yet there are two
One rich and warm, one poor and cold.

I am young, yet I am old.
I am weak, yet I am strong.

I eat, yet I still hunger.
I drink, yet I still thirst.

I love, yet I allow myself to hate.
I am used and often abused.

I am right, yet I am wrong.
I am human, but who cares?

But there is one thing that I know,
And this I can say with certainty.

I am not confused.

Tribute

By Johann "Hazael" Smith

My Mother's like
The closest thing to God that I've known.
I choose not to insult her with a card.
I see her when I ponder God.

Called out for Ma and met MA-AAT.
She shelters me in her wings.
No disrespect to my pops,
But her praises I must sing.

Her constant refrain,
See that my word meet my deeds.
Sire seed,
Must be there to see to their needs.

This wise daughter, taught by a Gray Fox.
I see that the spirit lives on
Even after that pine box.

She has sipped at the sometimes bitter Cistern of Wisdom,
Only to feed her Physical, and Adoptive children with The Pure Bread.

I love you MA – AAT.

Wedding Bells

By John H. Redd IV

Individual chords chimed to completeness;
The blessed harmony of a fated pair.

Tomorrow's wedding bells
Faintly resonate within my soul,
For me so distant... yet so close.

As each moment passes,
Becoming a fragment of history,
It introduces the growth of a glorious melody,
A melody that serenades forever.

Celestial sounds intoxicate reasons,
Reasons for Being;
Love, destiny and heaven... our symphony.

Pardon Me

By ZERAHKYAH!

Pardon me if I stare
And Pardon me if I dare
To share and bear my fantasies
Of rubbing my fingers through your hair.

Pardon me if I'm attracted
To your entire mental package
Or if I'm helplessly drawn
To the perfume you have on.

Pardon me if I happen to see
My future children in your eyes
And if I can't stop pursuing you
Until my hopes and dreams are realized.

Don't mean to offend
But I do intend
To cause broken hearts to mend
And rivers to bend.

Pardon me for wanting
To share love with you,
Constantly thinking of you,
Desiring to rise above with you.

Pardon me for wanting
To massage your back
Until the pressure of this world disappears
And the hot oil burns away your fears.

But I just want to put my arms around you
And surround you like the rings of Saturn.
Show you compassion with passion
And rearrange your thought patterns.

Would you hold it against me
If I held you against me
And squeezed you intensely
Yet ever so gently?

We could travel the cosmos
Going only where God knows.
We'd travel at light speed
And bring forth only right seed.

Create whole new planets
With mountains of granite
And beaches of black sand
As soft as your back hand.

I'd beg you to pardon me
As I make you a part of me.
It's only the art in me
That describes what you are to me.

Love is love, Love
From rubs to snug hugs
To much suds in tubs
Toes dug in plush rugs.

And I could write you a poem
That puts us back in the Garden
Somewhere right before
I found myself begging your pardon.

Break Free

By Donna Redd

Heat of summer,
Days too long.

Throngs of bodies
Peace gone wrong.

Idle minds,
Dreams unfulfilled,
Crack of gunshots.
Black baby killed.

Young Black men,
You fall as leaves from the tree.

Your youth, innocence, your future,
Have been crushed – will never be.

Look inside yourself – you know,
Life is a challenge.
Your heart, your mind might agree.

With love of self, guidance, discipline
And knowledge, you must – break free.

Satan

By Robert Redd

The Best things in life are truly free.
But that's not how it appears to be,
For imposed upon this reality
Is a normal system of insanity.

A world into which a young mind is bent,
But for just a short while Gods grace is lent.
After coming forth from noble birth
To spend but a short while on mother earth
Stands at the ready without a sound
To dash that new life to the ground.
To keep it bound with certainty
Like a force we know as gravity
To hover through life in misery
Bound to the world on bended knee.
Life's true pleasures never known.
Over this young heart weeds have grown.
Never knowing or having what's called a true friend
Except for the one who's called Satan.

Are You There?

By James Gardner

Has my mind started to wonder?
Why can't I find you?
My mind is racing.
I feel the pace quicken and my heart sputters.
My fingers stammer at the keyboard
Looking for the right word.
Are you still there?
Have I lost my opening?
Is it something I said?
Do you long for love?
Why can't you see me?
Questions race back and forth.
I want them to pop but…
Your humor
Your stance
You are too far away.
I want to pull you to me
Hold you in my arms
Kill the evil on the outside
Quell the storms that rage within.
I want you to be so much more than just a friend.
Accept my love.
Let us pick up where we left off and begin.
No reply from anywhere…
Damn, are you there?

Grown Men Do Cry

By Vernon C. Robinson

A beard and moustache cannot dismiss
The joy and pain that drips
Traveling downward that leave rivers
On my soft mahogany cheeks.
May be streams of speechless delight.
Could be of indescribable hurt.
But see I've already departed from my infant days
Those kindergarten moments,
Those teenage years
At the point where I could become
A mature father to a child
A wise husband to a woman
A responsible elder to some young cat on the streets.
Yes I'm a man and yes I have feelings too,
Ralph Tresvant-type sensitivity,
Bee Gee-type emotions.
And this human does supply quarts of teardrops
Despite what others may say.
Please don't be misled by pseudo thugs and roughnecks
Who claim to be too hard, too gutter, too hood to shed one
'cause inside every coconut shell
You will always find transparent milk of sentiment.
Didn't we witness Reverend Jesse after Obama declared victorious?
Or what about Eddie Levert after losing both his sons?
Remember Kevin Garnett capturing the Celtics' 17th world NBA championship?

I recall Hines Ward shed one after hearing Jerome Bettis calling it quits
Only to give the Steelers one last shot and won Superbowl XL.

Not all men can hold back tears like a beaver's dam.
Sooner or later our levees will break
And there's no need to point in laughter
Calling us punks, suckers and wimps.
Funerals...success...heartache...sad love songs
Machines that can cause one grown brother to break down
While a female might utilize her hand as a handkerchief
And erase the sobs away.
So the next time you hear someone say
A man ain't suppose to cry,
Tell them that's not a man
Because this man standing before you
Ain't ashamed to show his feelings
'cause it only proves that I'm human.

Happily Eva After

By Angela Shyr

I was making out with
Happily
Eva After
Because the taste
In my mouth
Was there,
All along -
It tasted so good
For that long -
All along,
This bump
I can't help
Sticking my tongue
On -
This bud,
A nerve ending
Over which
I can't help
Fawn -
This bud,
A reserve of tissue
That awakens
The dawn -
This bud,
Such pleasure
Could never
Ever
Possibly be
Gone.

Morning

By Hebert Labbate

Our bodies twisted together
Like bed clothes from last night.
The smell of flowers that lingers
Is coming from your thighs.

The covers are made of silk
Yet your skin is what I feel.
The sun reflects off the windowsill.
The whole world is standing still.

That is morning with you.
The day before the day starts.
My heart is warm and full
Of the light within your heart.

Give Your Self a Way

By Laurel Kilbourn

You can try to fool yourself into believing
That you are empowered
When you say you choose to give yourself away
Before you are stolen.
Yet you are not only fooling yourself.
You are also robbing yourself
Of the power you once owned within you,
The power to be...
Whole
Complete
Unbroken
Safe
Saved
Valued
Worthy of being who and how you are
Exactly as you are.
Believe this
For this is the seat of self-empowerment.

Untitled

By Eddie Neal

"Briapatch" - my term of endearment for the one
whose harmonious existence is dependent on her
ability and opportunity to create.
Whose peaks and valleys, progress and
Pain of the past have shaped her
Complicated persona.
I watch as she has struggled at times
To make sense of it all.
But like a beacon in a lighthouse on dry land
To wayward sea travelers on a stormy night,
The two she birthed - the real jewels
of her existence; her hopes and dreams of
their success and happiness guide her steadily
through any challenge she may face.

I admit - no easy feat to build on
What we have and grow.
For we, as one, with two strong
Views of life, are charged with
Passion, on the page and off.
We've been through IT - thick and thin.
But when the big screen clears, we
Actually mirror each other.
We love hard and live hard.
I call my queen Briapatch.
Warm, passionate, sensitive, caring, loving
And loyal on the inside.
Tough, prickly, unpredictable, combative,
and slightly weird on the outside.

Looking for Inspiration

By Lynette Gittens

In an attempt to take a direct path,
I walked and talked with me.
I was looking for inspiration.

On the open road to enlightenment,
I listened and heard nothing.
I saw and perceived nothing.

At the juncture of fulfillment,
I encountered truths, some I don't believe.
I sat and waited awhile,
Looking for inspiration.

And there it was,
Sitting with me
All the time.

Nobody Cries Like a Poet

By Brett McCall

Nobody cries like a poet.
Liquid, lyrical seeds soaking trees,
Only to sprout phonic fruitage
That the unknowing swear comes with ease.

No one cries like a poet,
Molding pain's darkness
Into pleasure's shade.
Bearing your own weakness for another heart's aid.

Not a soul cries like a poet,
Screaming in silence
But scribbling aloud.
Laying down line after line of your life on thin linen clouds.

Only a poet can cry like a poet,
And for us that is no surprise.
It is not being pretentious,
Just a fact that we cry with our hands and eyes.

But don't you cry for us poets,
For we would not have it any other way.
For it is in those moments of intense joy and pain
Where we find the words we so desperately need to say.

About the Author

A Boston native, Abria M. Smith embraced her love for the arts at an early age. She began writing poetry at age seven. Her love of creative writing led her to become a poet, lyricist, and playwright. At the age fourteen, she began her performance career as a singer and rapper, which eventually led her to earning a degree in Music Business/Management from Berklee College of Music and performing as an opening act for Busta Rhymes in Germany. Her poetry has been featured on the albums of recording artists, including Walter Beasley and used as the text for musical compositions. She is also a professional actor, working in film and theater. The importance of the arts in her life is best described by her signature statement, "When I cease to create, I cease to exist."

www.ingramcontent.com/pod-product-compliance
Lightning Source LLC
Chambersburg PA
CBHW021956290426
44108CB00012B/1093